GREGORY CORSO's first book of verse, *The Vestal Lady on Brattle,* appeared in Cambridge, Mass. in 1955, published by subscription by Richard Brukenfeld and a group of the young poet's friends at Harvard and Radcliffe. Later, in New York and San Francisco, Corso was associated with Allen Ginsberg and Jack Kerouac in the rise of the "Beat" movement. His famous "Bomb" poem (see foldout facing page 32) was first published in 1958 as a broadside by Lawrence Ferlinghetti at the City Lights Bookshop in San Francisco, where his second book, *Gasoline,* also appeared in the same year. *The Happy Birthday of Death* (1960) was followed by an extended period of travel and living in Europe—England, France, Germany, Italy and Greece. Some of this foreign experience found its way into the poems of *Long Live Man* (1962). Corso's first novel, *The American Express,* was published by Olympia Press, Paris, in 1961. The next three years were spent in the United States, mostly in New York, though for one semester Corso taught poetry at the University of Buffalo. His short play, *In This Hung-up Age,* appeared in the *New Directions 18* anthology. Corso returned to Europe in 1964 for two years, but is now living again in New York. His work, in translation, has been published in books, anthologies, and magazines in France, Germany, Italy, Czechoslovakia and a number of Latin American countries.

THE HAPPY BIRTHDAY OF DEATH

SALEABLE TITLES

Fried Shoes
Pipe Butter
Radiator Soup
Flash Gordon soap
Areopagus
Remarkable
Caesarean operation
Sterile Tunisia
Ashes
Cars are love
Earth is not even a star
Fearful compassion
A trembling of roses
Woe is me !
Coffee
Gargoyle liver
Jellies
Of all substances St Michael is the stickiest
Hairy abdomen
General indifference futilely thrown
Watermelon
The Deserted Desert
The Wet Sea
The Rumpled Backyard
Agamemnon
Treelight
The Happy Birthday of Death
Wrought reckless luke mood
All is permissible
A king is a very strange thing
Hail, Jack Falstaff !

The Happy Birthday of Death

GREGORY CORSO

A NEW DIRECTIONS PAPERBOOK

SIXTH PRINTING

For Stanley Gould
who remains and keeps on going.
G.C.

CONTENTS

THE HAPPY BIRTHDAY OF DEATH

NOTES AFTER BLACKING OUT

Lady of the legless world I have
    refused to go beyond self-disappearance
I'm in the thin man's bed knowing my legs
    kept to me by a cold fresh air
Useless and not useless this meaning
All is answerable I need not know the answer
Poetry is seeking the answer
Joy is in knowing there is an answer
Death is knowing the answer
(That faint glow in the belly of Enlightment
    is the dead spouting their answers)
Queen of cripples the young no longer
    seem necessary
The old are secretive about their Know
They are constant additions to this big
    unauthorized lie
Yet Truth's author itself is nothingness
And though I make it vital that nothingness
    itself will collapse
There is nothing.
Nothing ever was
Nothing is a house never bought
Nothing comes after this wildbright Joke
Nothing sits on nothing in a nothing of many nothings
    a nothing king

HOW HAPPY I USED TO BE

How happy I used to be
imagining myself so many things—
    Alexander Hamilton lying in the snow
    shoe buckles rusting in the snow
    pistol shot crushing his brow.
Behind a trail of visiting kings
I cried :
    Will Venice and Genoa
    give welcome as did Verona?
    I have no immediate chateau
    for the Duke of Genoa
    no African bull for the Doge of Venice
    but for the Pope !
    I have the hideout of the Turk.
    Informer? No—I'm in it
    for the excitement;
    between Afghanistan and Trinidad
    intrigue and opera are electrified
    everywhere is electricity !
The mad spinning ballerina
sees me in the audience and falls into a faint,
    I smile I smile I smile—
Or yesterday when I heard a sad song
I stopped to hear and wept
for when had I last imagined myself a king
a kind king with ambassadors and flowers and wise teachers—
What has happened to me now that
everything has been fulfilled?
Will I again walk up Lexington Avenue
or down it
feeling warm to Richard the Third
and the executioner
whose black hood is oppressive to wear?

Am I not music walking behind Ben Franklin
music in his two loaves of bread
and Massachusetts half-penny?
I knew 1768 when all was patched eyes and wooden legs
How happy I was fingering pieces of eight, doubloons—
Children, have you not heard of my meeting
with Israel Hans, Israel Hans—

SEASPIN

To drown to be slow hair
To be fish minstrelry
One eye to flick and stare
The fathomed wreck to see —
Forever down to drown
Descend the squid's conclave
Black roof the whale's belly
Oyster floor the grave —

My sea-ghost rise
And slower hair
Silverstreaks my eyes
Up up I whirl
And wonder where —

To breathe in Neptune's cup
Nudge gale and tempest
Feel the mermaid up
To stay to pin my hair
On the sea-horse's stirrup —

HAIR

My beautiful hair is dead
Now I am the rawhead
O when I look in the mirror
the bald I see is balder still
When I sleep the sleep I sleep
is not at will
And when I dream I dream children waving goodbye —
It was lovely hair once
it was
Hours before shop windows   gum-machine mirrors   with great
                                                          combs
pockets filled with jars of lanolin
Washed hair I hated
With dirt the waves came easier and stayed
Yet nothing would rid me of dandruff
Vitalis Lucky-Tiger Wildroot Brilliantine   nothing —
To lie in bed and be hairless is a blunder only God could allow —
The bumps on my head — I wouldn't mind being bald
if the bumps on my head made people sorry —
Careless God! Now how can old ladies cookie me?
How to stand thunderous on an English cliff
a hectic Heathcliff?
O my lovely stained-glass hair is dry   dark   invisible
not there!
Sun! it is you who are to blame!
And to think I once held my hair to you
like a rich proud silk merchant —
Bald! I'm bald!
Best now I get a pipe
and forget girls.

Subways take me one of your own
seat me anybody
let me off any station anyman
What use my walking up Fifth Ave
or going to theatre for intermission
or standing in front of girls schools
when there is nothing left for me to show —
Wrestlers are bald
And though I'm thin O God give me chance now to wrestle
or even be a Greek wrestler with a bad heart
and make that heart make me sweat
— my head swathed in towels in an old locker room
that I speak good English before I die —
Barbers are murdered in the night !
Razors and scissors are left in rain !
No hairdresser dare scheme a new shampoo !
No premature hair on the babe's pubis !
Wigmaker ! help me ! my fingernails are knived in your door !
I want a wig of winter's vast network !
A beard of hogs snouting acorns !
Samson bear with me ! Just a moustache
and I'd surmount governance over Borneo !
O even a nose hair, an ingrown hair,
and I'd tread beauty a wicked foot, ah victory !
Useless   useless
I must move away from sun
Live elsewhere
— a bald body dressed in old lady cloth.
O the fuzzy wuzzy grief !
Mercy, wreathed this coldly lonely head a crowning glory !
I stand in darkness
weeping to angels washing their oceans of hair.
There goes my hair ! shackled to a clumping wind !

Come back, hair, come back!
I want to grow sideburns!
I want to wash you, comb you, sun you, love you!
as I ran from you wild before —
I thought surely this nineteen hundred and fifty nine of now
that I need no longer bite my fingernails
but have handsome gray hair
to show how profoundly nervous I am.

Damned be hair!
Hair that must be plucked from soup!
Hair that clogs the bathtub!
Hair that costs a dollar fifty to be murdered!
Disgusting hair! eater of peroxide! dye! sand!
Monks and their bagel heads!
Ancient Egypt and their mops!
Negroes and their stocking caps!
Armies! Universities! Industries! and their branded crews!
Antoinette Du Barry Pompadour and their platinum cakes!
Veronica Lake Truman Capote Ishka Bibble Messiahs Paganinis
Bohemians Hawaiians poodles

'LET US INSPECT THE LYRE'

Like picking Orpheus' teeth !
I would not like to see humpsuch men
    gather about the instrument —
    baboons inspecting the backs of baboons.

Lilliputian afternoons !
Put to Uranian sleep only to wake
Creep through laughing bowl
    and drab populace cup
Snatch its grumpy tabernacle
    and grin its ingredients up
Thin inspectors sucking on sticks of thunder
— Greasers of angel wings.

Perhaps the strings *are* strings !
Yes. But they contend no fault in their hands.
The fault must be in the instrument
    (else in that inbetween mystery).

The king on his couch of victory
Seeks no spell but that of music —
    a fair-haired youth on his knees
    fingering thrice-wired air.

Stand on the Thracian stair !
Never see the new-born Siren
    bitch her chant imperfect —
Beauty's expression is eternal stead.

Faithless lyrists I have read
They'd amputate the rose to know the rose
    — and patch it a clumsy detection.

No thing of beauty was meant for inspection
Else detected
    it would blush
    and ache to endure

UNDER PEYOTE

The flower that bounces sneaking through a
door holding a girl from home
with
    a new light
   a bannister of music
The difference of minutes

    for

        summer
        children

       target

        bacteria

TRANSFORMATION & ESCAPE

1

I reached heaven and it was syrupy.
It was oppressively sweet.
Croaking substances stuck to my knees.
Of all substances St. Michael was stickiest.
I grabbed him and pasted him on my head.
I found God a gigantic fly paper.
I stayed out of his way.
I walked where everything smelled of burnt chocolate.
Meanwhile St. Michael was busy with his sword
hacking away at my hair.
I found Dante standing naked in a blob of honey.
Bears were licking his thighs.
I snatched St. Michael's sword
and quartered myself in a great circular adhesive.
My torso fell upon an elastic equilibrium.
As though shot from a sling
my torso whizzed at God fly paper.
My legs sank into some unimaginable sog.
My head, though weighed with the weight of St. Michael,
did not fall.
Fine strands of multi-colored gum
suspended it there.
My spirit stopped by my snared torso.
I pulled! I yanked! Rolled it left to right!
It bruised! It softened! It could not free!
The struggle of an Eternity!
An Eternity of pulls! of yanks!
Went back to my head,
St. Michael had sucked dry my brainpan!
Skull!
My skull!
Only skull in heaven!
Went to my legs.

St. Peter was polishing his sandals with my knees!
I pounced upon him!
Pummeled his face in sugar in honey in marmalade!
Under each arm I fled with my legs!
The police of heaven were in hot pursuit!
I hid within the sop of St. Francis.
Gasping in the confectionery of his gentility
I wept, caressing my intimidated legs.

2

They caught me.
They took my legs away.
They sentenced me in the firmament of an ass.
The prison of an Eternity!
An Eternity of labor! of hee-haws!
Burdened with the soiled raiment of saints
I schemed escape.
Lugging ampullae its daily fill
I schemed escape.
I schemed climbing impossible mountains.
I schemed under the Virgin's whip.
I schemed to the sound of celestial joy.
I schemed to the sound of earth,
the wail of infants,
the groans of men,
the thud of coffins.
I schemed escape.
God was busy switching the spheres from hand to hand.
The time had come.
I cracked my jaws.
Broke my legs.
Sagged belly-flat on plow
on pitchfork
on scythe.
My spirit leaked from the wounds.
A whole spirit pooled.

I rose from the carcass of my torment.
I stood on the brink of heaven.
And I swear that Great Territory did quake
when I fell, free.

DISCORD

O I would like to break my teeth
by means of expressing a radiator!
I say I must dent that which gives heat!
Dent! regardless the tradition of my mouth.

I would like to drive a car
but I must *drive* it!
Look — there must be a firing squad, yes,
but why a wolf?
I mean if I pass by with a rainball ball
should I pass by with a jackinthebox instead?
Confused I'd best leave wonder and candy and school
and go find amid ruin the peremptory corsair.

Sober
Wier Moors furs tails deer paws
risked and fevered thinking
owls in flashlight.

I HELD A SHELLEY MANUSCRIPT

(written in Houghton Library, Harvard)

My hands did numb to beauty
as they reached into Death and tightened!

O sovereign was my touch
upon the tan-ink's fragile page!

Quickly, my eyes moved quickly,
sought for smell for dust for lace
        for dry hair!

I would have taken the page
breathing in the crime!
For no evidence have I wrung from dreams —
yet what triumph is there in private credence?

Often, in some steep ancestral book,
when I find myself entangled with leopard-apples
        and torched-mushrooms,
my cypressean skein outreaches the recorded age
and I, as though tipping a pitcher of milk,
pour secrecy upon the dying page.

1953

Men! No good this matter of life and death. Flash
Gordon by a yellow cell knee up rifle on it — guards.
No chance his beautiful bullets hitting us.
So let's bring him lunch.
While he eats let's a magic so the prisonyard pivot
dull lifers from solitary.
A magic that our hands be fat to pray.
Let's a jolly havoc to rollbarrel pass topsy-turvey
heirs of zombic chairs and noosey trees.
Let us a magic so we be free to march Chagall-like
pass cowy warden and the turnkey his floaty keys
pass the P.K. his hooked nose
pass the trusty pass the stoolie — Men! Flash
Gordon is a kind illusion the final guardian
let's not slit his throat or stab his back
put away them sharpened tin cups.
He eats he'll give his back for us in thanks return
to leap from and bound over the yellow wall.
Come let's dash! hop leap! over!
For that free world I've no magic.
The little fear remaining in us will disappear.
Must we run for greater freedom? I've no magic.
Some of us have lost 20 years!
Forget it. Let's run pass the trees the human trees.
Ahead is ominous.
Beyond tree humanness that city
that birth of our crimes O can we freedom enough
to forget to atone our senile accusers or kneel before
our old forgotten arson or unstring our old bri . . .
Men! Let's bypass the city let us fly let us go jet
until we crash safely into snow from huge pink foundations
— gentle children await us.

Men! the penguin yawks are coming!
Arctic vision! Lid of earth!
We arrive may Emil hear the old shot he fired
I've no other magic to mercy his ear.
Why does Roger carry the electric chair on his back?
He's too old and Luis is old we old bastards finally free.

ON PONT NEUF

I leave paradise behind me
My paradise squandered fully
What dies dies in beauty
What dies in beauty dies in me —
Alone in this monk cell
I switch money from hand to hand —
With the wrong gate open
I hold a devileye on Red Mountain
— It's a warm evening
An afterrain from noon
Tonight I weep no loveliness
No love! — No love and love!
Cries of love! Cries of no love!
Blasphemies of the loveless!
Harmonies of the loved!
I'd a rope around my neck
A cold shake of music —
O what rang-a-tang crap now meaningless and wet
    beneath one of France's famous men's horses
        do I focus myself?

SPONTANEOUS POEM AFTER HAVING SEEN
THE METROPOLITAN MUSEUM

Three years since I last saw the wounded amazon
Central Park and I'm out here
         and old Greece is in there
What have I learned? That we're both under the hint
         and protect of Death?
Something I can't put my finger on. Those cat jars
         those clothy birds those chapters of slick men
    born in the year 1
Or why I smiled a know viewing Toledo — those
         cracking skysheets
         those skywalls spires turrets porticos skylent to
         green hills and bathers
Something more than God lies behind it all —
Fauns the happy noons the slow brools the sleeping berryfed
O lovely peacock don't hurt the monkey and his fruit
How long this Dutch perfection this twisted prophet
         this delicate forge for ivory tales —
Most to mind the time-cleansed air of murder
         the wood-carved brocatelle cubic orientation of Death
O ribboned haunching Sphinx and Hermes hat of prophecy
         I talk Death something we never talked
What faun? What noon? The white-haired weep!
         The young stand in awe
         Women fling their bodies!
I sharpen white on this my all-night
I grit Tiepolo headdress I bold poor heaven
What fanged demon squeak grace I've honed no place
         would destroy or teach me unnatural savour
Angelico's prayed hands still must pray and Hals
         musical smiles of state witness terse and spelled
That was Picasso! slipped eyes suddened in life still must see
         Death blindfold

   — beards on bald satyrd faces
I drive hard into a rare Phrygia King Midas King Gordius
The red-capped skeleton the Mr Death of 1465 looking at some
                plans

And the queen's head spilled gold and
Washington and Ri——
The whore doll of Asia leaned in to smile
The bull and the girl
The two crusaders and the girl
The girl and the horses of France —
That was a good museum that was a museum to see at night
I wish at night the alabaster throat the stoutest silver
the knightly chime the ringed Etruscan — yes! O
what good my sitting here and Greece in there
this writing and that marble gab
 — There's a jeweled mountain rolling down that child's nose
5th Avenue astiara astiara syconob bastiara
Look at me 1959 and still stupid about godknowswhat
the Tiglon is dead — the hunter never hunts
       hider never hides
       hunter catches all
       hider never hides
Hail! O splendid hunter in thy room of moldy nets!
from secret funnels I hollow ring thy name!
Hail! Hail! O Finder of all!
Every Rembrandt inspect!
Ha! and you gnome damned sneak midge!
Hider in the pickpocket of geepy Death!
Ha! Ha! Hider in nought!
Too much sun for the ant!
A million times more light I beg do focus on my ant future
Be this, this?
This museum parkstill smoke plaster dust enough equip for God
Copley! Copley! Cole! Sargent! Whistler! One day is
    sufficient to scream in the park or
   rush back into the museum
    and go see Bosch

and ask for — no no no no no no no
I should take the bus
The globe —
Were those shots? Everything adds dramaticly to delivery
of gunmen who take part in shapely revolutions because April
bears no conquest — I say I ate tar from the streets of summer
and one day is insufficient to scream I say one day while
chewing it I watched a gunman asleep on a bench drop his
grey Stetson I say O how to adjustalign —
A witche's bonnet a witch is on it I don't like his poetry anymore
Why not take the bus! Spring. My thinning wrists. My new
                                                      sneakers.

WATERCHEW!

He climbs the stair
The steps are old and carpeted   he climbs
He climbs the stair each step is another step
I sit on my bed   he climbs
I get up   bolt the door   put out the lights
I go to the window   I can't scream
I sit back on my bed with a smile   it's all a dream
A knock!
Hail Waterchew! big gubbling goopy mouth
Ho hairy clodbound oaf of beauty   hail!

I renounce the present like a king blessing an epic
I must beat the noon with a gold bassoon
In Waterchew I sleep Norse-proud
On ship deck furs I   O how deep into fear must I wedge
The strangeness I follow fools!

27

POETS HITCHHIKING ON THE HIGHWAY

Of course I tried to tell him
but he cranked his head
    without an excuse.
I told him the sky chases
    the sun
And he smiled and said :
    ' What's the use.'
I was feeling like a demon
    again
So I said : ' But the ocean chases
    the fish.'
This time he laughed
    and said : ' Suppose the
        strawberry were
            pushed into a mountain.'
After that I knew the
    war was on —
So we fought :
He said : ' The apple-cart like a
              broomstick-angel
      snaps & splinters
           old dutch shoes.'
I said : ' Lightning will strike the old oak
      and free the fumes !'
He said : ' Mad street with no name.'
I said : ' Bald killer ! Bald killer ! Bald killer !'
He said, getting real mad,
    ' Firestoves ! Gas ! Couch !'
I said, only smiling,
    ' I know God would turn back his head
    if I sat quietly and thought.'
We ended by melting away,
    hating the air !

MARRIAGE

Should I get married? Should I be good?
Astound the girl next door with my velvet suit and faustus hood?
Don't take her to movies but to cemeteries
tell all about werewolf bathtubs and forked clarinets
then desire her and kiss her and all the preliminaries
and she going just so far and I understanding why
not getting angry saying You must feel! It's beautiful to feel!
Instead take her in my arms lean against an old crooked tombstone
and woo her the entire night the constellations in the sky —

When she introduces me to her parents
back straightened, hair finally combed, strangled by a tie,
should I sit knees together on their 3rd degree sofa
and not ask Where's the bathroom?
How else to feel other than I am,
often thinking Flash Gordon soap —
O how terrible it must be for a young man
seated before a family and the family thinking
We never saw him before! He wants our Mary Lou!
After tea and homemade cookies they ask What do you do for a
                                                living?

Should I tell them? Would they like me then?
Say All right get married, we're losing a daughter
but we're gaining a son —
And should I then ask Where's the bathroom?

O God, and the wedding! All her family and her friends
and only a handful of mine all scroungy and bearded
just wait to get at the drinks and food —
And the priest! he looking at me as if I masturbated
asking me Do you take this woman for your lawful wedded wife?
And I trembling what to say say Pie Glue!
I kiss the bride all those corny men slapping me on the back

She's all yours, boy! Ha-ha-ha!
And in their eyes you could see some obscene honeymoon going
on —
Then all that absurd rice and clanky cans and shoes
Niagara Falls! Hordes of us! Husbands! Wives! Flowers!
Chocolates!
All streaming into cozy hotels
All going to do the same thing tonight
The indifferent clerk he knowing what was going to happen
The lobby zombies they knowing what
The whistling elevator man he knowing
The winking bellboy knowing
Everybody knowing! I'd be almost inclined not to do anything!
Stay up all night! Stare that hotel clerk in the eye!
Screaming : I deny honeymoon! I deny honeymoon!
running rampant into those almost climactic suites
yelling Radio belly! Cat shovel!
O I'd live in Niagara forever! in a dark cave beneath the Falls
I'd sit there the Mad Honeymooner
devising ways to break marriages, a scourge of bigamy
a saint of divorce —

But I should get married I should be good
How nice it'd be to come home to her
and sit by the fireplace and she in' the kitchen
aproned young and lovely wanting my baby
and so happy about me she burns the roast beef
and comes crying to me and I get up from my big papa chair
saying Christmas teeth! Radiant brains! Apple deaf!
God what a husband I'd make! Yes, I should get married!
So much to do! like sneaking into Mr Jones' house late at night
and cover his golf clubs with 1920 Norwegian books
Like hanging a picture of Rimbaud on the lawnmower
like pasting Tannu Tuva postage stamps all over the picket fence
like when Mrs Kindhead comes to collect for the Community Chest

grab her and tell her There are unfavorable omens in the sky !
And when the mayor comes to get my vote tell him
When are you going to stop people killing whales !
And when the milkman comes leave him a note in the bottle
Penguin dust, bring me penguin dust, I want penguin dust —

Yet if I should get married and it's Connecticut and snow
and she gives birth to a child and I am sleepless, worn,
up for nights, head bowed against a quiet window, the past behind
                                                              me,
finding myself in the most common of situations a trembling man
knowledged with responsibility not twig-smear nor Roman coin
                                                      soup —

O what would that be like !
Surely I'd give it for a nipple a rubber Tacitus
For a rattle a bag of broken Bach records
Tack Della Francesca all over its crib
Sew the Greek alphabet on its bib
And build for its playpen a roofless Parthenon

No, I doubt I'd be that kind of father
not rural not snow no quiet window
but hot smelly tight New York City
seven flights up, roaches and rats in the walls
a fat Reichian wife screeching over potatoes Get a job !
And five nose running brats in love with Batman
And the neighbors all toothless and dry haired
like those hag masses of the 18th century
all wanting to come in and watch TV
The landlord wants his rent
Grocery store Blue Cross Gas & Electric Knights of Columbus
Impossible to lie back and dream Telephone snow, ghost parking —
No ! I should not get married I should never get married !
But — imagine If I were married to a beautiful sophisticated woman

tall and pale wearing an elegant black dress and long black gloves
holding a cigarette holder in one hand and a highball in the other
and we lived high up in a penthouse with a huge window
from which we could see all of New York and ever farther on
                                               clearer days
No, can't imagine myself married to that pleasant prison dream —

O but what about love? I forget love
not that I am incapable of love
it's just that I see love as odd as wearing shoes —
I never wanted to marry a girl who was like my mother
And Ingrid Bergman was always impossible
And there's maybe a girl now but she's already married
And I don't like men and —
but there's got to be somebody !
Because what if I'm 60 years old and not married,
all alone in a furnished room with pee stains on my underwear
and everybody else is married ! All the universe married but me !

Ah, yet well I know that were a woman possible as I am possible
then marriage would be possible —
Like SHE in her lonely alien gaud waiting her Egyptian lover
so I wait — bereft of 2,000 years and the bath of life.

FOOD

Surely there'll be another table.
Whortdye spread on nepenthean beans;
Southernhorns alight on Hesiod carrots;
Hare visionary astrologer stew;
Talc and dolphinheart mixed kangaroonian weep;
Spanish knights brandishing piteous forks;
Dutch kitchens, rosy-cheeked cooks,
Still-life ducks and rabbits,
Piles of silver fish, vast orange pies;
Global Rex kettles volcanoing away —

The farmer will never love me,
He feeds me purposelessly.
I do not wish to eat
With the knowledge of his wheat;
Mine with the knowledge of love
Has put down his murdered meat —

Hunger! petty agent of Death,
If anything to mature me, *you!*
Five-day sister making paper of me.
Sadder than the Last Supper
I eat nothing
— Melancholy learns to starve.
And even if I did eat
— The hand from soup absurdity
Reaches the mouth's enameling;
There's not much loveliness in that.

Wisconsin provisions
Insufficient when I have absolute dairy visions:
Corduroy eggs, owl cheese, pipe butter,
Firing squad milk;
The farmer will never love me

Nor I, he.
I'd rather go hungry
Than assist his chicken slaughter,
Attend his State Fair,
Or screw his famous daughter.

Because restaurant eating is noticeable
And I am no longer that boy to lean against the window
And pick my nose mischievously;
Because now my eyes are sad on the plate
And envy the eaters their fabulous shriek of
SOMEPLACE ELSE LET'S EAT!
Yes, eat! Eat!
Hammer your pork chops with blows of love!
I mean, hammer your fantastic jowl!
Each swallow to roar the grace of your sweet fist!
The table must go!
Terrorize the smooth plates! The thick spoons!
O mummy roots! Stomachic dire of Thoth!
Augh! eat a steak of pine! A cut of spruce! Boil rock!
What else so dreadful a nourishment to wage a soul
Who dreams to beat an overseer to death
In a field of magnificent peas.

I am no sad hunter of what I eat.
It is for God to deny the foody ka of Egypt
The calf that never looks West.
And well I know some food is demonstrate of denial.
Osiris, I join thee! unnoticed in the calf's eye.

— Nice, 1957

Venice, 1958 —

I eat! and well!
I run to the ancient years
    and gather menu from potsherd —
Blue-mopped heads bake blood sweetness!
Ah, Venice feast!
Such the cuisine I am now exultant to eat!
Sugared meats! Badger tongues! Chinese lineaments!
I give ceremony to orangestuffed duck.
Vast fly, I shape thy shape for mouth shape!

The bard's oath is all a-moon; evening song,
Hat-feathered frolic mandolineer ho-ho!
Greyhounds staring beneath toe-bell feet —
Eat, eat! The table must go!
I rope my tongue! Gut my gut!
Goose legs stream from my eyes!
I plunge my hands into apegrease!
The plate avalanches!
Baked lions, broiled camels, roasted fennecs,
Fried chairs, poached mattresses, stewed farms!
O I have often sung to hosts of roast, much of song
Yet afraid to eat more —
Magical kisses for the cook who thrust me wild wheat!
Tonight a bed of straw; thankfulness, and a will to live;
I regain what I lose though I grow fat!

When this table goes
When the inevitable wolf enters the door
I'd not hesitate to music my eternal meal to the dew.

SHE DOESN'T KNOW HE THINKS HE'S GOD

He is God
John Rasin is God
He stands by the window smiling
watching a child walk by
' I am God ! ' he screams. He knows

His wife taps him on the shoulder
' John the baby is sick will die
His fever is up. Get a doctor.'

John Rasin stands as though he were dead
with the health and freshness of life
exaggerated in his deathness
He stands a man stunned with the realization
that he's God. He is God !

His wife pleads screams stamps the floor
pounds her fists against the wall
' John the baby will die !'

THE FRIGHTENING DIFFERENCE

The more I think Christ blood not blood
The blooding brow unlike the split forehead
    of a drunk who fell
the more I think of my own blood —

O how sad I get if even my nose bleeds !
I feel Christ bled easier
The way I have about His blood is not
    like the feeling I get when I see maybe
    a little blond girl sopping above the ear —

I don't seem to mind animal blood
The butcher's apron never scared me
And war's blood
even if each war caused an ocean of blood
    I didn't really mind —

And thank God I've never seen my father bleed
And my friends, thank God, only finger accidents —

I don't understand but
it's a good feeling I get
    a self-sad feeling when I spit blood —

But O, O how strange I felt when I saw
a tailor fall from his chair, a heart attack.
And a minute, just a minute after
    a trickle slipped from his mouth
    just a thin slip
    not like a stuck bull gushing
yet how more frightening the human line than the animal flow.

DEATH

1

Before I was born
Before I was heredity
Before I was life
Before I was — owls appeared and trains departed

2

Death is not a photograph
Nor a burning mark on the eyes
Everything I see is Death
Not Grim Reaper scythed and hourglassed
Scratch nor skullcrossbones
Nor bull butterfly

3

Call Death not a lesser name
Dead men I've known called Death less
A stubborn roar is a sad error
Nor valor once resuscitated be valor again

4

Owls hoot and the train's toot deflate
I beg for the breath that keeps me alive
Pitch I spew and pitch I wait
— A departed train is a train to arrive

5

The bitter travel is done
Take me Death into your care
I wait in the terminal
Exultant to breathe your avalanche air
My body's quilt hath spilt
I raise my feet

And the porter sweeps
What once was my meat

6

Death comes zoomed-hands like a storm
Whoa the tailcoats of old men !
Whoa aching futures !

7

O when I close my eyes
          the black I see is blacker still
          and when I sleep the sleep I sleep is not at will
          and when I dream I dream children waving goodbye

8

Desperate clinky tumult merging cank
Midnight dense slumber thaw
Gold murmurous silk pullman
Double townsmen
Polluted boot witchmaker bootmaker shoemaker
Dust crime
Dull budge
Stale lace
Irrigated casket
Purple lips flap message that breath is now alien
Death's laughing nose
Black week
Is dead side by side with cobbled hour
          is dead of building whirlwind shy centurions
          is dead windless mortal dry
          is dead uncomprehending harsh divorce from life
          to life to death and linger blacker week
          to succumbed year terrific obscurity a bitter trek
O this White War
This snowskull
This immaculate thaw

9

Hang all kinds of ailments cramps and shrieks away
Outflush allegoric atoms
Summon flexile agonies transfusions bloats and shrinks
Rekindle fire in a Browny café

10

There be a palace in Deathland
Deathchildren sapping in sunny porticos
Deathhorses nibbling deathgrass
Death king and death queen heralding a tournament of Death
There be the Deathslayer breathing cold fire
There be the knightly Death
Deathmaiden
Sound clarions ! combat
And all the dead be avenged

11

Let's all die
Let's practice a little
Let's play dead for a couple of hours
Let's everybody weave elegant everlasting cerements
       build fantastic tombs
       carve lifelong coffins
       and devise great ways to die let's !
Let's walk under ladders, cross the paths of black cats,
       break mirrors, burn rabbit feet, snip the 4th petal,
Yes ! let's draw the ACE OF SPADES —
Let's sleep with our doors unlocked

Hark witchen!
Envy the make of Death
Crank the earth
Jake the moss
Give weep for the right of tend
Filtrate the fierce soul
Hello the sook of night
Give should for need
Chance be it many sures are in the making
Merry lack!
Full-lept impervious jack!
Ox-flushings, scour'd malady, suffused sulphur,
Sepulchral ebb —

13

On to explore Death I go
Bragging old snowballs to Osnag Tragaro dumping
      Esufer Wolb in the snow
Trumpet in a satchel of Deaf I go
Soon on Death's bandstand
      I'll blizzard the ashed blow

14

Witch pickles dilled in broomsweat
Werewolf hair from Transylvanian bathtubs
Ho! the rosebee from its skeptical let
      eyes me as being unscientific —
O tail of Italian workhorse!
O abandoned farms!
Hear my formulae!
I have the way to bring back the dead
I have I have and love me for it
O I the KNOW of Death!
I dark mad ah solace dreams grace miracle quack awful O!

15

Drsxqo ! Pitchfork Blook fires chickens
    down a perilous road
Drsxqo ! have you a dead beast for me?

16

And the owl sobs
The vizer Croat
    is scratched a tally
Hear the owl rally

MEDIEVAL ANATOMY

Teeth are the castle gates of mouths
Tongues the dragons
Throats the dungeons
Noses the bowmen
Eyes the turrets of blonde maidens
Brains the lookout
    able to spot
    the treacherous **Black Knight** !

EARLY MORNING WRITINGS

1

The rooster at dawn
The hen asleep
— Frying eggs in a chicken coop

2

And this is Zeus
           a plucked pear
bitten into by an American child

3

A man crosses the street
I stand on the corner applauding him
— he made it !

4

By the hammer
By the blow
— the nail finds its way

5

The taxi stops at the 42nd Street library
— I don't understand

6

Two men look into each others eyes
— one shoe is missing

7

Beams of a gold insurrection
— coughing against huge pillows

8
The mother's talk
The child's ear
— the plans of a kingdom burn

9
Thank God for Longhi
        his black cloaks
        and three cornered hats
        and long nosed white masks
— A bird looks like me
        flying over the Monoprix

10
My little niece forgive me
In the noon cursed wind
        I can't be an uncle

DREAM OF A BASEBALL STAR

I dreamed Ted Williams
leaning at night
against the Eiffel Tower, weeping.

He was in uniform
and his bat lay at his feet
— knotted and twiggy.

' Randall Jarrell says you're a poet !' I cried.
' So do I ! I say you're a poet !'

He picked up his bat with blown hands;
stood there astraddle as he would in the batter's box,
and laughed ! flinging his schoolboy wrath
toward some invisible pitcher's mound
— waiting the pitch all the way from heaven.

It came; hundreds came ! all afire !
He swung and swung and swung and connected not one
sinker curve hook or right-down-the-middle.
A hundred strikes !
The umpire dressed in strange attire
thundered his judgement : YOU'RE OUT !
And the phantom crowd's horrific boo
dispersed the gargoyles from Notre Dame.

And I screamed in my dream :
God ! throw thy merciful pitch !
Herald the crack of bats !
Hooray the sharp liner to left !
Yea the double, the triple !
Hosannah the home run !

NO DOUBT WHAT HE SAW

Who doubts the horse's dynamite teeth
when the inevitable daisy like a bit is gripped —
A flower not to explode
            but loaned to the image
                hanging chewed from the mouth's side.
Who'll doubt it will not dangle there
and become ancestral to the makeup?

Lying beneath a tree, 13, half naked,
I had long been fixed in its dynamite eye —
Staring back at it I did not explode
nor did my playmate who doubted it all.

Side-stepping cow flop
he plucked wild apples singing fun at me
and returned with three
giving me the rottenest.

I led him by the hand from Crest cottage
            down Lincolndale Road
and there, in a field of burning hay,
no doubt what he saw —
A pastoral metamorphosis!
A Daisytaur.

WRITTEN WHILE WATCHING
THE YANKEES PLAY DETROIT

Between the banks of life and death
the spheres will be known
and we'll be elected to solar palaces
and we'll fall on one another
and ride the freighted light
and repentance will keep us gay
— our humanness left like a mouse-tear in a knot.

Creation licks our blood, what can we know?
A sort of shadow, a warped cluster, a sad foliage?
The mystery of life is in the Recorder's craft :
Two one-eyed Scythian frogs wreathing deer
and with them go the firebirds the old flowers
the magnificent monsters unicorn and Dionysius
and the King's final crier on the whirling rug.

Between the banks of life and death
obsessed symbols curl with decrepitude
the unteachable genesis the struggling stream
physical orchestral the apex balance of Thermopylae
we'll compare ourselves to apparitions death and masks
we'll a charred humor and spidered smile
we'll a terra-cotta soul all whitened parochial
we'll a signalled grief, or is it old twig scrawl?

Creation licks our blood the spheres are ours !
Houses of home yeowd like drooling plowmen
the pestilent reflect the frail lake of a duck
brickies yawning front porch gossip

O Homesteader sink the board! threat the spineplank!
fold up furious gone-goblin!
have door and window terrorrun the world is done.

Beyond the banks of life and death
to neighbal dominion bridge and harrow
whiter rugs than ever to fingerrun
we'll be sick for want of library swag.

Creation fumes our blood
where to stuff the butler awful like fuel?
Downstairs in yesterday's room fire crept from fireside
and beamed a senate of rolling lions
to out the door yard hunk junk crab meal spring fig.

A LITTLE LOST

Immortal goat
ring your good bell;
with God's ear loaned
I eavesdrop near —
Ring! bright crier
the Vast to hear.

48

GIANT TURTLE

— from a Walt Disney film

You rise from the sea an agony of sea
Night in the moonlight you slow the shore
Behind you webbed-tracks mark your ordeal
An hour   in an hour you cease your slow
Hind legs now digging   digging the sand the damp the sand
The moon brightens   the sea calms
Your mouth pumping   your eyes thickly tearing
You create a tremendous hole   you fall flat
Exhaust   sigh   strain
Eggs   eggs   eggs   eggs   eggs   eggs   eggs   eggs   eggs
Eggs   eggs   eggs   eggs   egg   egg   egg
Heave   exhaust   sigh   flat
Your wet womb speckled with sand   you turn slow
Slow you cover the hole the eggs slow   slow
You cease your slow
Dawn
And you plop in the sea like a big rock

A DREAMED REALIZATION

The carrion-eater's nobility calls back from God;
Never was a carrion-eater *first* a carrion-eater —
Back there in God creatures sat like stone
— no light in their various eyes.

Life. It was Life jabbed a spoon in their mouths.
Crow jackal hyena vulture worm woke to necessity
— dipping into Death like a soup.

FOR K.R. WHO KILLED HIMSELF
IN CHARLES STREET JAIL

Death's cruelest day!
Night places its lapsed headdress
        on the shelf of heaven.
Bald confusion! Nothingness pavilioned!
By what light follow reaping demons
        toward
            down
                cathedral secrecies
        illuminating the wet straw cell where
            an old woman in her childhood dies?
Hag of youth! Infancy bone!
Down in death gather light from human windows!
Eyes are self-consumed
Light is the bone of eyes —

The teats of Lethe sucked by that one poet I knew
His illuminated rose of pain grew in such a light —

O bring down the stars and swop their trinklets of light!
Force down the angel of humancy
        and bayonet it
            in the light!
By light follow, O child of dark, by light embrace!
    Here
        touch my electric hand.

PARANOIA IN CRETE

Damned Minoan crevices, that I clog them up!
Plaster myself away from everything, all that out there!
Just sit here, knees up, amid amphora and aloe,
reading lusty potsherd, gobbling figs, needing no one —
Mine the true labyrinth, it is my soul, Theseus;
try a ball of string in *that*!

Thrones descended by kings are ascended by ruin;
upon no singular breast do I rest my head of mythologies;
no footman seat, no regnant couch, enough this pillowy cave —
O Zeus! I was such a king able to mobilize everything!
A king advised by oraclry his aulic valets imperium;
not kingsmen, nor my sons, that pederast Miletus;
that hot-shot Rhadamanthys, his nine year cave advocacy —
And my wife! that wood-cow brothel!

Clog! Clog! Clog! Stuff-up the cracks!
They'd like to dump me in a miserable nymph's bubbling brake!
Vise my feet in the River-god's mouth!
Perplex my head with Naiads!
Set Eros on me, that sequesterer of mortal vanity!
O Calypso's green-fluid boudoir is tearing me to pieces!
Plaster! Plaster! Stay the Aegean tide! Blot out Athens!

I survey the hunched bull, the twin headless lions,
one more crevice to go, and lo!
I forfeit the Echinadian Isles —

CLOWN

1

Laughter dies long after jest
The joker smiles no joke
A clown in a grave
Pranksters weep in Purgatory
Laughter dies long after jest
Joy
Bella, the memory of the heart
Yet the face is a joker smiling no joke

2

Like the jester who blew out candles
tip-toeing in toe-bell feet
that his master dream victories
— so I creep and blow
that the cat and canary sleep.

I've no plumed helmet, no blue-white raiment;
and no jester of-old comes wish me on.
I myself am my own happy fool.

As there are no fields for me to dedragon
— impossible to kneel before ladies
and kiss their flowery gowns.
I can only walk up and down hands behind my back
dreaming dungeons and spikes and squeaking racks.

For commoners, I put things on my nose
and tip-toe with the grace of gold.
For those I love I sit sad by stained glass
— all my face the mystery of some joke.
And for God I am ready with a mouthful of penguins.

I lock myself away!
I wash myrtle-birds in the sink.
Yes, I myself am my own happy fool
— stale with dreamless jokes.

Do I care? Yes I care. I want to make laugh.
O if only I were a winding toy
or just a winter bunny
        in a huge imbecile's pie.

I know laughter! I know lots of laughter!
Yet all I do is walk up and down hands behind back
dreaming dungeons spikes and squeaking racks.

3

And why do they say be a man, not a clown?
And what is it like to be a man?
I can joke like a saint for my need,
give in return for a goose-leg, a glow;
I need never know this joy I grease through life
or claim on woe substantial diet.
Fat if I want to be fat!
So easy to ice one's humor
— to fan the sun.

It is time for the idiot
to pose a grin and foot on the dead lion
(the embodiment of the clownless man) —
Time to grow a mustache; suck gin;
and win the hard-to-get lady.
Time to return from star trek
and scrub the earth.

Where am I in wilderness?
What creature bore my bones to this?
Here is no Eden — this is my store :
Rooms! Rooms! Electric lights!
A giant ocean on each shore.

Am I the man to jack-in-the-box
each misfortune of man, be it sickness
death or simply an unhappiness?
That man? That old clown
        with bent hat and tubed beard?
That looney tearfully recalling
        his rainbow ball?

No! Boot the jack of clubs into devildom!
Turn somersaults in the circus-coffin!
Mr. Death has the hero by the balls!

— I can commemorate black laughter, too.

4

I still don't know if the clown should die;
there's yet the black greyhound, the lioned battle axe;
the champ of heaven leaning against a cloud
        with crossed feet;
and the doomed myth
        centered in man war.

If there were no clown
but demoned whiskers shaking pale blue flowers;
if there were no smile
no climb of cherubim with lute and horn
no silvery chest, no suncast jug, no basin for swans,
not the delicate forge itself;
I doubt the reward of Paradise
to be a place where happy old friends meet.

54

If the clown were dead
the month of August would be weighed
        with sacks of sour wheat.
Dead the clown, there'd be havoc!
The angel's jeweled apse
        would collide
        and smash a ray of doves!
Fauns would lay waste the wood
        with faun-chewed babes!
Oily melancholy fits the black boot
now that the clown thinks to die.
Men the size of islands
        sink their joy in the helpless protect of Death.

O the whole tragedy! the weight of it!
with complaints to laughter not come —
Tickle then the clown to sleep for sleep he needs;
glum days poor America bares —
Old America could tell of laughter often as clowns tell —
Ben Franklin, W. C. Fields, Chaplin, the fat of joy!
Their happy light is forged phalanx, charge!

Snakes search the skies for flying rabbits;
monkies draft jackels — is the clown dead?
I grieve to futures a fishy grin,
for as I am I gloom of history.
A comical corruption! Death's indeathity!
The clocked tower's scythed chime
bodes sorrow and the life of man equal time.

5

Proud boastful buffoon! at full your fancies
swing swift youngyear to oldyear.

Is it for Death you rend black profit,
this meagre vanity deserved me?

It is life has flawed my gentle song;

sad intelligence examples my secret rich behavior,
o foremost physician at my dying side.

Good tricker! I distinguish your twisted floors
your ribboned furniture, your anguished doors.

Ho! you good mad pest of joy!
I won't stab your eyes with night,

or place a watchman's apey grapple
to nab you with his moral tickle.

You are not laughable
You have never been laughable
You have always been you, clown!
— a graft of lunacy on heaven's diadem.

Yet I die in thee;
fill your heart my tomb —

Forgive me, lovely one;
o there's that in me wishes each laugh
would knit an eternity of hilarity!

No, I shan't crowd your brainy grave;
it's enough I climb your jolly ladder
and have planets kick dust in my eyes.

Don't despair kind child of joy,
you'll get to God
and ease His dreadful tightrope.

6

The punches of winter knocked out a herd of deer.
Winter left the wood like a plate of chicken bones.
The naked clown shivers by the snowy brook;
the sleeping bear wakes to mock his bony blue legs.
Hold on, clown!
Every stone is cosmos;
every tree made of laughter stuff.
Paint wide your mouth white!
With elm leaves make fake ears!
Redden your nose with lizards!
Be ready!
Spring will soon step out from behind a tree
        like Eve from the side of Adam.

Tang-a-lang boom! Fife feef! Toot!
Spring welcomed by Barnum parade clears jammed melancholy
— traffic of a laughless age.
Mothers break their backs getting out winter babies.
Children climb daringly
        and sit with shirtsleeves on the shoulders of statues.
Cherry blossoms swell joy in the hearts of the old.
Girls skip, boys gather, dogs bound, cats leap —

Spring!
Good to go to the East River
and sit before Brooklyn
        with fresh knowledge of Hesiod on farming;
good to be intent on Alcman's *Maiden Song;*
sit good for hours re-learning
        the craft of classical verse —
Welcome Epinikian ode!

Yo! Yo! Myths of calamity
        announce heat heat by noonlight
        grains and berry-bees!
Elves bring handfuls of Spring
                to the dying winter king;
the old Crinch berry poisoned
        will soon be dead
        will soon be dead.

I knew you'd come, wild architect!
It's you I want; o heartily I laugh!
Why continue to bother about the profane ransom of Rome
when there's you? let the Turks and the missing noses of Greece
roil on the bottom of the Ottoman's grease pot.

Yo! God! Go ye snowdogs and fumigations!
Unlike the fauns on the banks of the Tiber
there's nursery for this age's cloven feet.

Winter, that I've been your clown;
that I've read your beady scripture
— I hold no grudge.
My joy could never wedge free
        from sorrow's old crack.

To the unicorn cling, failing
unlaughable lover of man; your red nose
is antideath —

A jerk of March you are —
Born in mockery, o that crazy month!
But born in mockery like all men
            from the womby head of a cheapskate,
a stingy creep who got great kicks
out of not telling you when and how and why life.

Enough. To the unicorn.
The clown's allowance of joy to man is useless.
Man is glued to sorrow and there is no escape.
All your slapstick gold . . . useless.

Go! cling to the unicorn with faked ears and tufted hats
— you'll never shake Death's laughter of mercy, poor nut!

Clown!
Homeless clown in Serious!

8

Of course the unicorn will be killed
so don't think your red nose
your flabber mouth
your million dollar laugh won't.

Of course the circus will mourn.
The fat lady they'll mourn less.

You made kids laugh to make money
so don't think you're a golden clown.
The time you cursed an acrobat
the time you refused a beggar
the time you cried.

Ah, it's not the circus clown I sing;
not the tumbling midge before the conqueror
        made to dance before horses,
not the Joker whose arsenal teeth
        explosively haw-haws out of jams;
no, nor is it the Tricker in whose hand the rope ends.

9

The comedy gone mad!
Poor clown, the weather of sorrow.

The clown's house FOR SALE!
        Crying bricks and porch
        Rotting door and windows
        and neat slopes of buttercups.

This night the finished clown
his stumps flash on gypsy caravan.
The swinging lantern objects his leaving home.
He's a phantom to crystal;
to ears he's hairy batter;
the hag's future glimpse
scarce allows him identity.
The moon garments a cloud;
the last wagon baits two trees;
he catches his ruffled neck
— whoa! his goopy scent!
Birds gulp his amulets baubles and trinklets.

The clown is dead!
Pass along the highways of 1959 — all clowns are dead!
See the great dumps of them swarmed by seagulls;
   their tufted hats frayed
   their face noses and ears smoldering
   their polka-dot coveralls darkening
    underneath the sun-fairy's final nighthorn.

The helly ringmaster cracks his whip!
The circus's great mercy shoots fire!
Acrobats gnaw their wires!
Skeletal apes twist meatless bananas!
The lion trainer's bony jaw
   clanks on the lion's bony jaw!
Hotdogs and coca cola for the charnel!
Elephant trickdust on the purgative scale!
Fifty shrouded clowns pile out
   from a tiny tomb.

10

But
I am an always clown
and need not make grammatic
   Death's diameter.
Death, like a monkey's tail,
wraps down spirally on a rising,
   ever rising pole.

How to climb and sit on the turret
away from the breath of the sick
away from the souls who sleep
   in Death's cylindrical kick —
Ah,
   this surfeit of charlatanry
will never leave my organic pyx
   thank God

AWAY ONE YEAR

I think of New York City lost in stars
forgotten as a bluehaired pet of childhood love —
Tonight the night is full;
the stealthy Mayor in his fine discipline
moves in proportion like a large jewel with furry feet;
he taps his long straight nose through the years of his term,
a ghost with worry-thoughts of city —
Beneath the Washington Square arch he feigns to forget
the new denunciations of the day.
This has never been the Mayor of my city,
occasionally stopping in a barren area
with magnificent foundations in his eyes.

I have not promised blessing upon leaving Gotham gate;
in lovelier cities I join my dreams in whose care I depend
though not once owning love to any city but the city of my heart.
New York City. It is fierce now; chariot-locked in the sky
like a stag scraping its back against mountains.
Fierce as a doleful vision, giving piteous grammercy.
In a dying cat's Egyptian eyes
the lovely mouse is a man of dreams, so my city :
dreamy solace of rivers and bridges brightly onionskinned in the
                                                                    night

Down many urchin avenues
I see the days of my city bearding its face
its measure of skeleton clanking like a stove
the shell of Death come to navigate a city to the tomb.

ON PALATINE

Via Sacra I look down upon you,
my ownself tribunal,
before six-columned Saturnus
and tri-graced Castor and Pollux
— I see in dreamy barrage,
on pain-echoed Rostra,
an emperor's furled toga
swarmed by spined crawlers
— In the pool of the Vesta
I see a Brooklyn gang of war
heaped dead and neglected
— Behind me,
beneath sunflashed Titus,
a catechist of my youth
demands I return to America
— Is that my prison friend
smashing his fists against
the pillars of Jupiter?
— O God! God!
I'll never see things as they are!
Debauched of dream,
I've an eye impure for sight;
I dare not visit Greece.

A MOMENT'S WISH

Riding on the New Haven Line
Suburbia gave me a good feeling of winter.
I would like to have sat in that child's backyard
— the lovely winter of that!

PARK

In this park
    the children speak Italian
and do not
    mind the naked statues
as did the children
    who spoke French in another park
    making jokes at Hercules.
But the same with all children in all parks
    — bouncing balls with yawns.

The park is mad !
The old man eating his lunch takes hours !
Five nuns : spies !

    I draw a tree
    Children look behind me
    And do not
        mind the demon I put in the leaves.

The first drunk enters
    he gets the sunniest spot.

    Another week and Spring.
    Can't see that more leaves will help these trees.
    But more sun won't be refused.
    They'll probably paint the benches.
The park is quiet !
Where are the nuns?
The old man is still eating his lunch.
O God ! the mothers have abandoned their carriages.

But I've been in madder parks.
	Central Park was mad; Prospect Park even madder.
Ah, Washington Square Park : The whiskered chess players
The man with a doll scotch-taped to a turtle
Poodles Afghans Danes leashed Siamese cats going to the bathroom
Path of junkies gesticulating the universe with finical hands
Poets painters bongoists creeps bums Negroes
	sitting in the circle
	looking up at the pantieless girls.

He's finished his lunch.
I've finished drawing my tree.
But when are the mothers going to come back?

	Bronx Park, the zoo !
	The penguins : the Emperor King penguins
	the Humboldt Ringed-neck penguins,
		and the Komodo Monitor !

I guess I'll spend the Spring in Paris again.
Cemeteries are just like parks. Even better.
Of course the cemetery in Paris (the big one)
	is not as pleasant as the one in Charleston,
	not as quiet, and not as many trees.
But at least in a cemetery you won't find
	old men eating eternal lunches
	or mothers leaving their baby carriages.

In the park of God there are no children.

THE SACRÉ-COEUR CAFÉ

The fierce girls in the Sacré-Coeur Café
bang their wines on the table
screaming Danton triumphed having denied liberty
While the garçon demands Murat triumph on all that triumphs.
The bombed Algerians observe each others' burning teeth.
A scarey café the Sacré-Coeur Café.
The proprietors are like the proprietors in Les Misérables.
Always making me feel like Jean Valjean when I go there.
Thank God I've no sack of silver no yellow ticket to show.
But that's why I go there an ex-convict with no lodgings
sitting in a wooden corner eating black bread
waiting for little Cosette — the size of eternity.
Wait there that I follow her out into the night
that I might carry her water buckets
buy her a huge glorious doll
and take her far away
that she love me
that I carry her lover on my back through sewers
that I old and grey die at their wedding table.
Ah but there are plastic tables in the Sacré-Coeur Café.
The fierce girls all work in the Post Office.
The proprietors have no Cosette but a big fat son
who sits dunking croissants.
And the Algerians
they don't go to the Sacré-Coeur Café.

GARGOYLES

The gargoyles trumpet Paris to me
when it rains out of their mouths
    For centuries the same tremulous
petrified sepulchre cries
all into the Seine's narrow ear
    It's the way they're placed
    Outstretched gargy necks
screammouthed   haunched pensivity
blasting golden era echoes from cathedral nests
as though avenging   I imagine   speechless Quasimodos
    My ear is unlike the ear of the Seine
    In my ear more resounded unsepulchre birds
loom the sphere   the pinioned dome that is mine
this dream frontier   the brief flight   the zoomed utterance
that is mine to hear
    O I don't know what to think when they sit
like spies with no clothes   with no real eyes
watching me in the rain   gushing storms like a defiance
    They too would like raincoats
or something   I don't know   yet enough to know
their image false   their purpose contagious   counterfeit
I cannot feel that demondrains benefit the houses of God
on a rainy day   forbidding or decreeing nourishment for
                  the river's diet

FOR BUNNY LANG

There in the greater light
in the trembling urgency of the night
I see a dead music
    pursued by a dead listener.

WRITTEN IN NOSTALGIA FOR PARIS

How lovely that childgirl was!
The street was wild with raiders
    but France protected their youth.
I ran to buy her a flower but a rioter
    needed blood for the FLN;
    St. Michel sold the flowers
    but it was cut off by
    the Garde républicaine.
I ran up Notre Dame and called to an eagle
    that I might glide its eyes
    upon the childgirl's whereabouts, -
    and did! Wings to my eyes
    I sightsailed down the sad Seine
    and saw her mightily stand
    against the fish-hooks of the fishermen.
Angel of fish! I called! It was she the child!
The harp of carp, the flute of fluke,
    the brass of bass
    the kettle of turtle
    the violin of marlin
    the tuba of barracuda
    hail whale!
That I have followed beauty — reward to know
    there's a God for fish
I echo the prayers of all seas.

MORTAL INFLICTION

I think of Polyphemus bellowing his lowly woe
seated high on a cliff
sun-tight legs dangling into the sea
his fumbling hands grappling his burnt eye
And I think he will remain like that
because it's impossible for him to die —

Ulysses is dead
by now he's dead
And how wise was he
who blinded a thing of immortality?

FROM ANOTHER ROOM

Dumb genius blows
feeble breath into my windowless room
He — the sagacious mute
rap-tapping a code or doom
— the drunkard punched the wall to have his storm!
Through the crack! Through the crack!
My feast was in the easy blood that flowed.

69

LOOKING AT THE MAP OF THE WORLD

Germany has lots of meat
O what a treat !
Yet I thought of monkey meat
And dared not eat.

Holland has beautiful blond children
Different than Brueghel's children
Who are cheruby potatosacks

Sweden has sinister schemes to create
the airports of Space and Time

St. Paul's of England
is God's men's room

France has created the *weird* guillotine

Italy has given beauty to the world

Spain where the cult of bloodsteam
roils sad gayety

Monaco is useless to the world.

Mexico is enslaved in the Ten Commandments
— the brighest catch of God

America is the most promising of empires
— stamp collectors will have to re-geminate
their American albums

Venezuela had a dead man on the shore

HEAVE THE HIVE WITH NEW BEES

The dead a wildcold body must bear
Follow through with fineries
— an exact mandate
Sick and violent the senses
regain the catch old feelings difficult to rejoy

Sursum corda O dead ! With a bragged requiescat
spray blood Deathdrench the dash of life

The dead are born in Cheeryland
Their buttocks neigh

OWL

Finicky bird of day,
I've never seen you;
never got that close.
If I did, would you click your great eyes at me?
God if only I could hold you close;
kiss you;
crush you goodnight.

ALL LIFE IS A ROTARY CLUB

Today's hide is sample of the inside skin
The inside skin is vanity   vanity is lovelessness
            vanity is another death
To think is vanity   to live is awful vanity
Yet the speeding spark of man presents respect to man
            All man is ONE in this sad
                        inharmonious weird predicament

Man in a forest away from man
The leafage lay low   greenjoy engrossing like a cloud
            reaches into noon and spreads a black choir
Dream steps down from a chessboard sky and conducts
the oratorio certain to bare the love of man a ball of snakes
            All man is ONE in this sad
                        inharmonious weird predicament

I walked with a man   He crossed streets like a panther
He didn't seem to mind bakeries   He had a nice home
            but didn't invite me in
I hid in his cellar filled with rat-chewed books
and by furnacelight read of creatures seeking a truth
            All man is ONE in this sad
                        inharmonious weird predicament

I heard a human say to a human be human
My imagination wondered the monster in me
            that thing in man other than human
The basher of heads   the schemed immolation
        Each being self-contained ensapphired

SATYR'S CHANT

This bright knife halves Greece from Rome
Sarpedon from Antinous — the mutual drear.

Slice the arms Turk-wise and let museums
Claim the rest — the mutual drear.

Correct Popes whacking away at marble cocks
Barbaric sameness — the same drear.

This blade wedges Daffy Duck from Sphinx
A similar oraclry — a similar drear.

Pegasus idle symbol I dissever one wing
Two wings apart — yet equal drear.

Surgical this knife to cut the spell from Achilles heel
The proposed arrow rots — still there's drear.

Split the centaur in two that half man and half beast
Be all — yet twin drear.

Knock off the caryatid's pedimental burden
Atlas has equal hold — equal drear.

This knife aimed at Zeus might do the trick
— I've enough dread.

SPRING'S MELODIOUS HERALD

She needs more attention than inanimate
paintings or a cat stuck in a tree —
Three years she's kept out of sight
And now she appears
    postponing the joy of my eyes.

I would attend her, stunned as I am,
more than my wounds; donate a rare red wine
that her company be parasitic —
She has appeared
    burning at my charity's jargon.

She needs my attention else another
Three years she'll be dead from my eyes
lost among the civets and globes of nature
a bitter trek for me to snout —
O watchful mercy! she hasn't disappeared.

Lovely lady with your kind guitar
twanging away at some great occasion for tender lambs
I'd as soon be part victim if but a wretch
that listens only to idle my wet eyes on you —
Play on, overwearied nurse, enfranchised in Spring.

Primordial melody tides triumphant O maniac lute!
Winter's vast network is set upon by hot wolves!
Snow-burnt my bloody shoulders aflapped with wounds
yet pursued by that cruel weather freezing every rosy good in me
O play on, wild fallow! broach my sleet ears with ambient coals.

Come, fire, my savage pet, come! purge my folds
with your crackling kiss that I tend your avalanche breasts
and prove pilgrimage toward that splendor you herald.

POWER

for Allen Ginsberg

We are the imitation of Power
Every man is to be doubted
There is no mouth no eye no nose no ear no hand enough
The senses are insufficient
You need Power to dispel light
Not the closing of an eye

Since I observe memory and dream
And not the images of the moment
I am become more vivid
And need not open the eye to see
With me light is always light
How powerful I am to imagine darkness !

Since I depend on heroes for opinion and acceptance
I live by proper truth and error
SHAZAM !
O but how sad is Ted Williams   gypped and chiseled
All alone in center field
Let me be your wise Buck Rogers !

Since I contradict the real with the unreal
Nothing is so unjust as impossibility
Outstepping myself as a man in Azerbaijan
I forge a rocket lion
And with a heart of wooing mathematics soar to passion a planet

O but there are times SHAZAM is not enough
There is a brutality in the rabbit
That leads the way to Paradise — far from God !
There is a cruelness in the fawn
Its tiger-elegance gnawing clover to the bone

I am a creature of Power
With me there is no ferocity
I am fair   careful   wise and laughable
I storm a career of love for myself
I am powerful humancy in search of compassion
My Power craves love   Beware my Power!

Know my Power
I resemble fifty miles of Power
I cut my fingernails with a red Power
In buses I stand on huge volumes of Spanish Power
The girl I love is like a goat splashing golden cream Power
Throughout the Spring I carried no Power

But my mission is outrageous!
I am here to tell you various failures of God
The unreasonableness of God
There is something unfair about this
It is not God that has made Power unbearable   it is Love
Love of Influence   Industry   Firearms   Protection
Man protected by man from man   this is Love
Good has no meaning and Sympathy no message   this is Love
THINK signs will never give way to DREAM signs   this is Love
We are ready to fight with howitzers!   this is Love
This has never been my Love
Thank God my Power

Who am I that sing of Power
Am I the stiff arm of Nicaragua
Do I wear green and red in Chrysler squads
Do I hate my people
What about the taxes
Do they forgive me their taxes
Am I to be shot at the racetrack — do they plot now
My monument of sculptured horses is white beneath the moon!
Am I Don Pancho Magnifico Pulque no longer a Power?

76

No I do not sing of dictatorial Power
The hail of dictatorship is symbolic of awful Power
In my room I have gathered enough gasoline and evidence
To allow dictators inexhaustible Power

I *Ave* no particular Power but that of Life
Nor yet condemn fully any form of Power but that of Death
The inauguration of Death is an absurd Power
Life is the supreme Power
Whoever hurts Life is a penny candy in the confectionary of Power
Whoever complains about Life is a dazzling monster in the zoo of
                                                                Power

The lovers of Life are deserved of Power's trophy
They need not jump Power's olympics nor prove pilgrimage
Each man is a happy spy of Power in the realm of Weakness

Power
What is Power
A hat is Power
The world is Power
Being afraid is Power
What is poetry when there is no Power
Poetry is powerless when there is no Power
Standing on a street corner waiting for no one is Power
The angel is not as powerful as looking and then not looking
Will Power make me mean and unforgettable?

Power is underpowered
Power is what is happening
Power is without body or spirit
Power is sadly fundamental
Power is attained by Weakness
Diesels do not explain Power
In Power there is no destruction
Power is not to be dropped by a plane

A thirst for Power is drinking sand
I want no song Power
I want no dream Power
I want no driven-car Power
I want I want I want Power!

Power is without compensation
Angels of Power come down with cups of vengeance
They are demanding compensation
People! where is your Power
The angels of Power are coming down with their cups!

I am the ambassador of Power
I walk through tunnels of fear
With portfolios of Power under my arm
Look at me
The appearance of Power is there
I have come to survey your store of Power — where is it
Is it in your heart your purse
Is it beneath your kitchen sink
Beautiful people I remember your Power
I have not forgotten you in the snows of Bavaria
Skiing down on the sleeping villages with flares and carbines
I have not forgotten you rubbing your greasy hands on aircraft
Signing your obscene names on blockbusters
No! have not forgotten the bazooka you decked with palm
Fastened on the shoulder of a black man
Aimed at a tankful of Aryans
Nor have I forgotten the grenade
The fear and emergency it spread
Throughout your brother's trench
You are Power beautiful people

In a playground where I write this poem feeling shot in the back
Wanting to change the old meaning of Power
Wanting to give it new meaning my meaning
I drop my unusual head dumb to the true joy of being good

And I wonder myself now powerless
Staggering back to the feeble boys of my youth
Are they now lesser men in the factories of universe
Are they there compressing the air
Pumping their bully profanities through long leafy tubes
I see them perched high on the shelves of God
Outpecking this offered hemisphere like a crumb —
O God! what uttered curse ushers me to them
Like a prisoner of war . . .
Be those ominous creaks of eternity their sad march?

How powerless I am in playgrounds
Swings like witches woosh about me
Sliding ponds like dinosaur tongues down to my unusual feet
To have me walk in the street would be *both* unusual

                                    — 1956

1958 —
Power is still with me! Who got me hung on Power?
Am I stuffed in the grizzly maw of Power's hopped-up wheel
Will I always be like this   head in   legs out
Like one of Ulysses' men in the mouth of Polyphemus
Am I the Power drag? Me   the Power head?
Just what Power am I for anyway!
The seized bee in a blaze of honey Power —
The spider in the center of its polar veil
With a fly-from-another-world Power —
Good noon nap on adoration lap with all cozy cruelty Power —
Towering melt like an avalanche of glass never ending chirring
                                      Power —

Stooped and hushed Chronicleleer of Spenserian gauderies
Is surely maybe my Power —

Whenever I play the fiery lyre with cold-fingered minstrelry
A luscious Power gives me a heavened consequence good as
                                              sunlight —
Awful blank acreage once made pastoral by myths
Now abandoned to mankind's honest yet hopeless
Anthemion-elixir is in need of my Power —
But the Power I have I built with my own help !
That bad wolf approach in dim-divine disguise Power
All mine ! All illumination sheep Power !
That woodsy savant fetch-eyed scarce perspective from
Balm-volumed epics that prouds shy fantasy my Power !
That hand-grenade humor dropped down the hatch
Of an armoured suit my proposed bit come doomsday Power !
O joy to my human sparkle Power !
Joy to its march down the street !
Ha ! The envy of diamonds in the windows !
The child of Power is laughter !

October you fat month of gloom and poetry
It's no longer your melodious graveyard air
Your night-yanked cypresses
Your lovely dead moon
It is October of me ! My Power !
Alive with a joy a sparkle a laugh
That drops my woe and all woe to the floor
Like a shot spy

ARMY

Thrice I've seen the two-gunned ghost of Patton
waxing wars in the backroom   whitehaired and mad
his fat thumbs pressing violence with schoolboy gaud.
He hates God he has alchemy cannons aimed at Him!
Badgered angels (wine-soaked rags) slaughtered by his orders
by his battalions of exorbitant drunks
hang (not as sweet Alexander would have it hang)
like rags in the bombblotched air of God.
Yet . . . those who die most courteous
do become the dreadful applause in any great decline.
Remember,
trembling aristocracies   doomed
laughed to slay flies.

I think of war mythical wars
flowing from the wrinkled mouths of bards
wars that defile tears
uplift horrible iniquities
plunge complaints in noble speech
turn white the infant hair of the world
wars that go mad
that banish the leaking ox   the stuck pig   the pinned swan
wars that drink blackberries
wars that pee behind the hideous shack of Farm
wars wars wars
war : A blessed hour
stole from the heaven of God.

I left the imagination army
stricken by the penitential muster
over my shoulder a swollen gun —
I made my way to instant wars
my medals were laughing faces
in my hand I held a diploma of Rifle

Ah what war next? I stood on the threshold
my army-gloved hand, its woeful knock,
provoked the door of Peace;
Athene requests my unbecoming.

I stepped upon an old bombardment
my path pyloned by dark meditative Generals.
' So!' I cried, ' So this is the sadness of Generals!'
I sat awhile in the arms of Eisenhower and slept
and dreamed a great bomb had died,
its death rattle made Stentor
in the breast of my human bed.

I ran down the bombarded fetch of war
North of Rzhev
in the bend of the Don
on the hump of Stalingrad
outrunning the German General Staff
fled from Rostov (confused)
the only exit the Kerch Straits
now where? now where?
Beyond the Crimea
— a lonely dark wet wicker basket.
O the basins of the Don
the Volga
the great bend of the Don
Generals Vatutin Golikov Kuznetsov
Leliushenko
How can I love the Army?
Doves honk it wicked!
Nothing I know wishes a young man die
(perhaps Army)
One concise bullet aimed at the heart
can never separate youth from youth
(perhaps Army can)

Even with all its helmets
who can love the Army?
(Army)
Army walks the battlefield and does not retreat
Army kneels before the boys who fell and
revels in the fragrance of their gunpowdered mouths
Army likes to hieroglyph the ground
with fragments of lyric youth.
How can I love the Army?

From foxhole illusion where I sit
secretly drawing pictures of my mother
I know I am but a stupid boy waiting to be shot
Yet no thing I know in man wishes me die.

They said shoot the young boy and I did.
I would like to have shot him at a distance
They had me put the pistol to the back of his head
I cried
but the army summoned the brass band
(its prestige and morale supply)
and soon my sobs became song.

That war gives me chance
to breathe air appreciatively
        is wonderful
That I may die with all my beautiful hair
        is not forbidden
That I no longer dream of Jane or my cats
but of Flying Fortresses
        is forgivable
That I can tear the faces of youth
That I can char their heads
That I can give them smoking knees
That I can

Army you dirty rotten — O my heart!
I know you'd like me to make friends
with my fellow soldiers
but I'll not!
Tonight when attack screams us back into infancy
I'd not like to hear them bullet-torn tell me :
' Death is a consuming blackness '   how dull!
I've heard that in all your other wars.
How sad the first buddy I took by the hand in death
who, in words of blood, said :
' That a soldier can't die a unique death is lamentable '

Rommel leads Hollywood across the Sahara
Montgomery flees!
Zhukov clumps like the baths of Caracalla into Berlin
Rundstedt hides in the bombed opera house
his shiny boots gathering dust in the back room of Gigli
Guderian examines with tears in his drooping swastika eyes
Ukrainian pitchfork wounds in his mistress tanks
Eisenhower yanks out appendix
thus to lead healthy wealthy and wise the whole shebang!
And miles and miles away Shades MacArthur
wets his knees in tropic water
the mangled children of Buddha floating pass his eagled belly
                                        button.

Battalions! Platoons! Garrisons!
In everywhere they go they war
hand in hand
their promises mutual
their hearts faulty
In everywhere they go they kill
some carry diaries
some, poems
everyone reads a sacred prayer

Army's sacred prayer
Holy be to Papa Patton who leads us
into the poolrooms and brothels of War!
Holy be to Papa Patton, he'd never fight Nebuchadnezzar!
He leads us fatherly martherly gartherly into
Death! Death! Death! Death! Death!
Bullets in our blue eyes, holy be to Patton!
Grenades in our bellies, Patton!
Tanks over our bright blond hair!
O Harpo Death and thy clanking harp, hear!
Holy be to Patton he gives hills to Death!
Army! Army! Army! Army!

POLICE

Yes! one momentflash BANG — and boiling boywar
One moment be it gang or burglary or rooftop sleep
torches a solitary shattered surprise — just one moment
a whiff only, a boybelly ripped by 38 divinity —
The desk sergeant goes mad to place pennies on the eyes
to hear at night in sleep dizzy hyenas moaning aerial laughter
Starmeat, them cops'd eat starmeat; take a seat by God
Sit by God, they'd sit and order more of themselves —
Horned Reality it's snout ringed with tokens of fear
pummeling child's jubilee, man's desire,
was never meant in the dove-model of things —
Police will shrink crisp thank new worlds O God
O corrupter shrink! shrivel as would a stabbed leech
Shrivel with you all your billioned bluecoats brassbuttons
clear smooth the earth
— hosannah the swimming feet of Beauty

Though anger does not remain the countenance of a dreamer
or vengeance the dream
the thought of beauty encourages

Tell me of police heaping hill-berries
sticking fingers in stone ears — giggling happy dangers
Police! bare heaven lugs away dark dereliction!
Men sin on snow, their souls acrid
the death they cast returns;
the critch of electric chair tames the beast,
and rain pindells its hock-head fate
a bolt strikes the heart no less extravagate —
Death! jump while the skully pie-wagon rolls
Prat on the monotony-backs of cops and robbers
crash their lips together — kiss!
Death! send forth thy compassionate mother to yank

86

the billy out of the hand —
Life! St. Francis all police!
Demand golden stoolpigeons on their shoulders!
Black Seraph stigmatize John Law!
John Law kneel in the midst of God!—

    Sun on the brush
    Beasts in the cave
    Sleeping snakes
    Temptation clowns
    Thin trees
    Tiny mushrooms

Ah but Death's wheeled-skull rolls
Youth and the breakers of life look up forever
Raptured sound fountains twinkling lemons
O all that policelight!
Kneel, too, delinquency!
Kneel to God midst His making!—

    Mossy badges
    Gnarled nightsticks
    Dry 38's

Forever delinquency look up!
Who does John Law refuse? No one.
Law never takes away the sun.
Enter Law's chamber; brag old snowballs to Law;
Law can make winter eternal
Spring temporary; yes, consider Law.
Law will sanctify all you've done.
Law is not only charity, Law is magic!
Love Law. Follow Law, obey!
Bang on Law's door.
Every inch of Its room is covered with floor.
Children present Law a bombsite!

Afford Law a bomb.
Give Law churches factories railways!
Restore terribleness unto Law's eyes!
Children, the fault is yours! Yourselves restore!
All is lamb-agony! The bleat is Law's!

O Police! debauched of boywar,
boybites on your flatfeet,
there is no lasting killer, all is figurative kill;
and murder washes away, flooddeath, deluge,
the dead the sad permanence the durable sadness —
Weep your shrill tears O police!
Blow your whistled requiems;
bark at human promise.

Green purged gatey plumed discolored Youth
who dumped you down the sewer like a petty gangster's gun?
The boys are in heaven, they are sad, there is no sadness there;
is there no sadness to tell?
The boys are swimming in the ocean of heaven,
can police reach their play?
But police too must go to heaven!
That's why the boys are sad
so sadly dancing
so tiredly kissing God —

Cop! forgive the cop-killer!
The mercies of man rivet heaven to earth —
Yes yes O cop go out into a field alone & see & know & feel!
There is no cop-killer in Beauty —
The Mad Dogs! The Esposito brothers! I was 11 years old
And my father only read the Daily News the Daily Mirror
and it was my mission to buy them
and I sat on the fourth landing of my building
and looked at the Espositos on the front page

their knees on the railway station ground
their white shirts up to their breasts
their handcuffed hands wringing like Christ crucified in the air
the mad dog tears in their eyes
the foam
and surrounding them the great cops of determination
and before them the great black train of determination
and in the train past wooded deer-second upstate New York
with its twin lakes and rush rivers and little summer towns
the electric chair —
I trembled on that landing and vowed I'd never be
those Esposito brothers but came close
and ran to my father and gave him his daily read
and he read it like he read yesterday's
I knew then nothing could save the Mad Dogs
And I knew with certainty that nothing could save any man
when I saw Rosalind Russell a female reporter
record for the Chicago Chronicle the death of a gas-chamber

                                                                   man —

Newspapers and films abandon the doomed
that even children cast their innocence to agree
— anyway I did at that age agree.
My father's indifference, Rosalind Russell's stardom,
the great big circulation of the News, the Mirror,
I praised the police their backing, their fame —
Henry Hudson screamed on the Half-Moon :
' Police are a necessary evil !'

I dreamed a cop, an old cop,
a whitehaired cop bowed sad on a sofa
knowing in his years he carried a gun
a gun to stop the breath of a breathing being
a gun to cause man to push up daisies forever —
And when that realization mowed him down on the sofa
— he wept to know man

1959

Uncomprising year — I see no meaning to life.
Though this abled self is here nonetheless,
either in trade gold or grammaticness,
I drop the wheelwright's simple principle —
Why weave the garland? Why ring the bell?

Penurious butchery these notoriously human years,
these confident births these lucid deaths these years.
Dream's flesh blood reals down life's mystery —
there is no mystery.
Cold history knows no dynastic Atlantis.
The habitual myth has an eagerness to quit.

No meaning to life can be found in this holy language
nor beyond the lyrical fabricator's inescapable theme
be found the loathed find — there is nothing to find.

Multitudinous deathplot! O this poor synod —
Hopers and seekers paroling meaning to meaning,
annexing what might be meaningful, what might be meaningless.

Repeated nightmare, lachrymae lachrymae —
a fire behind a grotto, a thick fog, shredded masts,
the nets heaved — and the indescribable monster netted.
Who was it told that red flesh hose be still?
For one with smooth hands did with pincers
snip the snout — It died like a yawn.
And when the liver sack was yanked
I could not follow it to the pan.

I could not follow it to the pan —
I woke to the reality of cars; Oh
the dreadful privilege of that vision!
Not one antique faction remained;
Egypt, Rome, Greece,

and all such pedigree dreams fled.
Cars are real! Eternity is done.
The threat of Nothingness renews.
I touch the untouched.
I rank the rose militant.
Deny, I deny the tastes and habits of the age.
I am its punk debauché. . . . A fierce lampoon
seeking to inherit what is necessary to forfeit.

Lies! Lies! Lies! I lie, you lie, we all lie!
There is no us, there is no world, there is no universe,
there is no life, no death, no nothing — all is meaningless,
and this too is a lie — O damned 1959!
Must I dry my inspiration in this sad concept?
Delineate my entire stratagem?
Must I settle into phantomness
and not say I understand things better than God?

New Directions Paperbooks

Henry Miller,
  Stand Still Like the [...]
  NDP236.
  The Time of the A [...]
  The Wisdom of the [...]
Yukio Mishima, *Conf* [...]
  NDP253.
  Death in Midsummer. NDP215.
Eugenio Montale, *Selected Poems.*† NDP193.
Vladimir Nabokov, *Nikolai Gogol.* NDP78.
New Directions 17. (Anthology) NDP103.
New Directions 18. (Anthology) NDP163.
New Directions 19. (Anthology) NDP124.
New Directions 20. (Anthology) NDP248.
Charles Olson, *Selected Writings.* NDP231.
George Oppen,
  Of Being Numerous. NDP245.
  The Materials. (SFR) NDP122.
  This In Which. (SFR) NDP201.
Wilfred Owen, *Collected Poems.* NDP210.
Nicanor Parra,
  Poems and Antipoems.† NDP242.
Boris Pasternak, *Safe Conduct.* NDP77.
Kenneth Patchen, *Because It Is.* NDP83.
  Doubleheader. NDP211.
  Hallelujah Anyway. NDP219.
  The Journal of Albion Moonlight. NDP99.
  Memoirs of a Shy Pornographer. NDP205.
  Selected Poems. NDP160.
Plays for a New Theater. (Anthology)
  NDP216.
Ezra Pound, *ABC of Reading.* NDP89.
  Classic Noh Theatre of Japan. NDP79.
  The Confucian Odes. NDP81.
  Confucius to Cummings. (Anthology)
  NDP126.
  Guide to Kulchur. NDP257.
  Literary Essays. NDP250.
  Love Poems of Ancient Egypt. Gift Edition.
  NDP178.
  Selected Poems. NDP66.
  Translations.† (Enlarged Edition) NDP145.
Philip Rahv, *Image and Idea.* NDP67.
Carl Rakosi, *Amulet.* NDP234.
Raja Rao, *Kanthapura.* NDP224.
Herbert Read, *The Green Child.* NDP208.
Jesse Reichek, *Etcetera.* NDP196.
Kenneth Rexroth, *Assays.* NDP113.
  Collected Shorter Poems. NDP243.
  100 Poems from the Chinese. NDP192.
  100 Poems from the Japanese.† NDP147.

[...],
  [...] *of Manhattan.* (SFR)
  [...] *e United States 1885–1890.*
  [...]P200.
  [...] *, Illuminations.*† NDP56.
  [...] *l & Drunken Boat.*† NDP97.
Jean-Paul Sartre, *Baudelaire.* NDP233.
  Nausea. NDP82.
Delmore Schwartz, *Selected Poems.*
  NDP241
Stevie Smith, *Selected Poems.* NDP159.
Gary Snyder, *The Back Country.* NDP249.
Enid Starkie, *Arthur Rimbaud,* NDP254.
Stendhal, *Lucien Leuwen.*
  Book I: *The Green Huntsman.* NDP107.
  Book II: *The Telegraph.* NDP108.
Jules Supervielle, *Selected Writings.*† NDP209.
Dylan Thomas, *Adventures in the Skin Trade.*
  NDP183.
  A Child's Christmas in Wales. Gift Edition.
  NDP181.
  Portrait of the Artist as a Young Dog.
  NDP51.
  Quite Early One Morning. NDP90.
  Under Milk Wood. NDP73.
Lionel Trilling, *E. M. Forster.* NDP189.
Martin Turnell, *The Art of French Fiction.*
  NDP251.
Paul Valéry, *Selected Writings.*† NDP184.
Vernon Watkins, *Selected Poems.* NDP221.
Nathanael West, *Miss Lonelyhearts &*
  Day of the Locust. NDP125.
George F. Whicher, tr.,
  The Goliard Poets.† NDP206.
John Willett, *The Theatre of Bertolt Brecht.*
  NDP244.
Tennessee Williams,
  The Glass Menagerie. NDP218.
  Hard Candy. NDP225.
  In the Winter of Cities. NDP154.
  27 Wagons Full of Cotton. NDP217.
  One Arm & Other Stories. NDP237.
William Carlos Williams,
  The Autobiography. NDP223.
  The Farmers' Daughters. NDP106.
  In the American Grain. NDP53.
  In the Money. NDP240.
  Many Loves. NDP191.
  Paterson. Complete. NDP152.
  Pictures from Brueghel. NDP118.
  Selected Poems. NDP131.
  White Mule. NDP226.

(SFR) A New Directions / San Francisco Review Book.   † Bilingual.

**Complete descriptive catalog available free on request from
New Directions, 333 Sixth Avenue, New York 10014.**

POE

SIXTH PRIN

T

F DEAT

ms by

EGORY CORS

"Bomb" as a fold

as been much p
the leading liter
e "Beat Generatio
ick Kerouac, Al
illiam Burroughs.
as been one of t
ie "Beats" from t
lmirers of his poe
gs quite as much
traditions in wo

s the revival of p
an "original"—be
hitman—has brok
e conventions to g
agic of language. A
ent pre-occupation
of the immediacy
n or Dylan Thom
e to the mystery
ips, his central the
ons ranging from t
comic are sounde

But Corso is seldom macabre. A bursting vitality always carries him back
the sensations of living, though always it is the reality behind the obvio
which has caught his eye.

"How I love to probe life," Corso has written. "That's what poetry is
me, a wondrous prober. . . . It's not the metre or measure of a line, a breat
not 'law' music; but the assembly of great eye sounds placed into an i
spired measured idea."

[Other books of poetry by Corso: *Long Live Man*, NDP127, $1.60; *Gasolir*
published by City Lights, San Francisco, $1.00.]

*Cover design by Rudolph de Harak. Cover photograph courtesy
of Brown Bros. Photograph of Gregory Corso by Howard Smith.*

A NEW DIRECTIONS PAPERBOOK   NDP86 $1.5